Wolfbane
BOOKS

KENNETH PADGETT and his wife, Rebecca, live in the South Carolina Lowcountry with their two young daughters. Kenneth is a PhD (cand) in Biblical Studies at Trinity College, Bristol (UK). He also holds a Master's degree in Old Testament from Gordon-Conwell Theological Seminary. He cherishes cool weather, a good Irish breakfast tea, and a pipe tobacco with a pleasant room note.

SHAY GREGORIE is a native of Mount Pleasant, South Carolina, where he lives with his wife, Catherine, and their nine children. He holds a Master of Divinity degree from Gordon-Conwell Theological Seminary, is a business owner, and an ordained pastor in the Anglican Church of North America. He eagerly awaits the day each of his kids can read *That Hideous Strength* and fully understand why he calls their home St. Anne's.

AEDAN PETERSON is an illustrator and visual developer born and raised in Nashville, Tennessee. He's been busy for the last few years, illustrating the new edition of *Pembrick's Creaturepedia*, The Tree Street Kids books, and *Dead-Eye Dan and the Cimarron Kid*. He's also delved into the world of animation working as a character designer and background artist for *The Wingfeather Saga* animated series. When he's not painting trees with his wife or playing with his daughter, he can often be found intensely overanalyzing some animated kids' movie.

Copyright © 2023 by Wolfbane Books

Published by
Wolfbane Books
1164 Porcher's Bluff Road
Mount Pleasant, SC 29466
www.wolfbanebooks.com

Cover and interior illustrations by Aedan Peterson
Cover and interior design by Brannon McAllister
This book was made by human hands, hearts, and minds.

Hardcover edition ISBN: 978-1-7366106-4-0
First Edition

Printed in China
10 9 8 7 6 5 4 3 2

THE
STORY
of GOD
Our SAVIOR

Written by
KENNETH PADGETT
& SHAY GREGORIE

Illustrated by
AEDAN PETERSON

For my mother, from my earliest memories you have shown
me the wonders of mending mercy and loving kindness.

—KENNETH

For my Mom, who for years sang His praises from our piano,
and now forever does the same before His throne.

—SHAY

For Mama, thanks for your kind friendship, and for
your relentless example of Christ-likeness.

—AEDAN

*We'd like to extend a special thanks to Nathan Wingate for his great comments,
suggestions, and edits as we were finalizing the manuscript for this book.*

Has anyone ever told you that the world is broken? That things aren't quite right? Of course, you already know this.

You feel it in your heart when you cry in pain, weep in sadness, or hurt the ones you love. You see it in the bright lights of an ambulance when it races down your street. You hear it in cold, angry voices when friends argue.

Was the world meant to be this way? Will it always be so sad? Is there a way that anything good can come out of all the bad?

There is! And that's exactly what this story is about, so be still and listen closely.

The story you're about to hear is meant to stay deep in your heart.

It's the healing story of a world that seems to be falling apart...

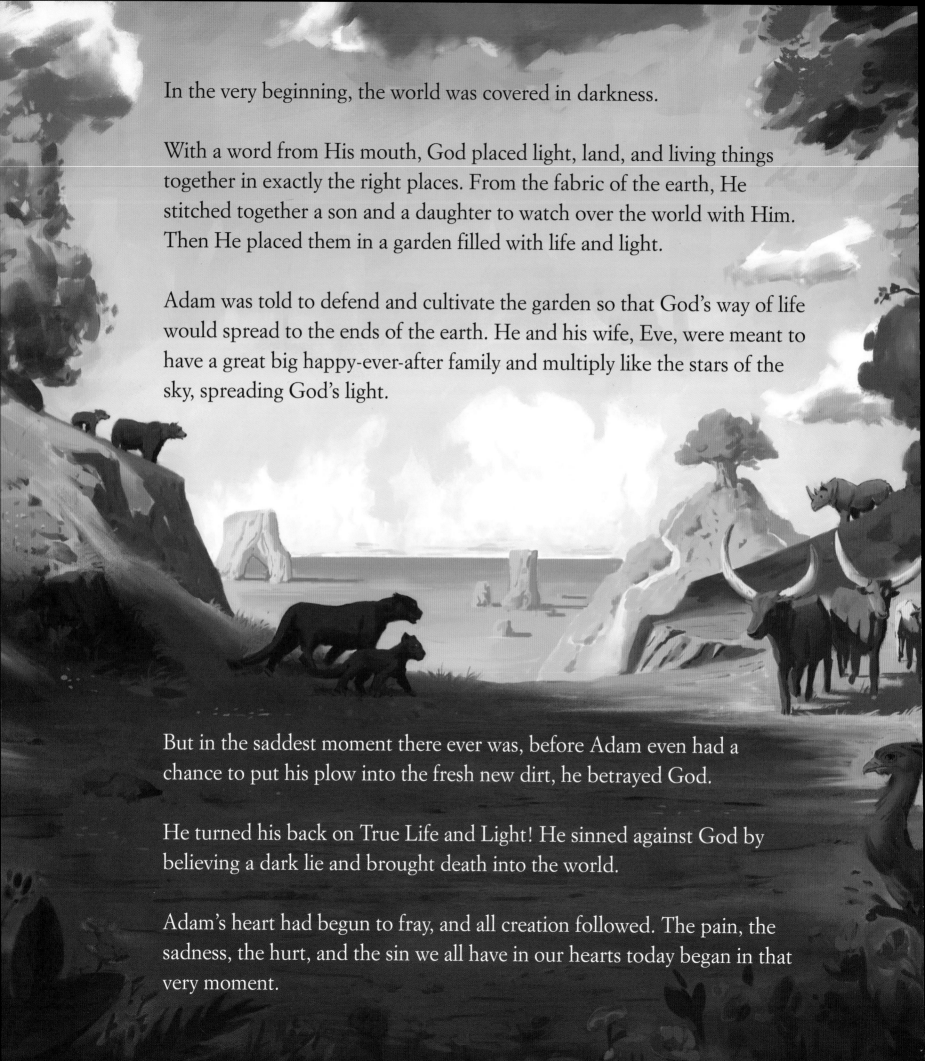

In the very beginning, the world was covered in darkness.

With a word from His mouth, God placed light, land, and living things together in exactly the right places. From the fabric of the earth, He stitched together a son and a daughter to watch over the world with Him. Then He placed them in a garden filled with life and light.

Adam was told to defend and cultivate the garden so that God's way of life would spread to the ends of the earth. He and his wife, Eve, were meant to have a great big happy-ever-after family and multiply like the stars of the sky, spreading God's light.

But in the saddest moment there ever was, before Adam even had a chance to put his plow into the fresh new dirt, he betrayed God.

He turned his back on True Life and Light! He sinned against God by believing a dark lie and brought death into the world.

Adam's heart had begun to fray, and all creation followed. The pain, the sadness, the hurt, and the sin we all have in our hearts today began in that very moment.

Even though they had done great wrong, God graciously covered their shame with garments made from an innocent animal. Then he sent them out into the wilderness with the promise that one day a distant daughter of Eve would give birth to a Son who would succeed where Adam failed. He would shine forth God's life and light to every dark corner of the world.

He's abounding in love,
  a Savior who mends!
Always and forever,
  world without end!

Even with God's promise of light, the world grew darker.
The unraveling of the human heart continued.

So He flooded the land, washing away all the works of those
who had betrayed Him.

But God's heart was for much more than this. In His great mercy, He saved one family, bringing them safely through the waters into a **new** beginning—a fresh start!

He's abounding in love,
  a Savior who mends!
Always and forever,
  world without end!

But the fresh start after the flood was a false start! Noah and those who came after him betrayed God just like Adam.

Was the human heart broken beyond repair?

Pain and sadness grew and grew.

It seemed like the unraveling of the human heart would go on forever! But those who knew God knew better.

A hush fell over God's army of angels. The waning stars and the weary world leaned in closely, hoping for words of healing.

Then without any warning, in a moment of mending mercy, God spoke to a man called Abraham.

"I have chosen your family! I will raise up one of your great-great-great-grandsons to be a Savior. He will bless all the families of the earth and heal their hearts so that they will be broken no more…"

"...But know this: Before that day comes, your family will be slaves for 400 years in a land not their own. I will hear their cries and rescue them. I will carry them through the deadly darkness into life and light."

Everything God promised came true. And just as He said—
God heard the cries of Abraham's family.

One still and sleepless night, with their sandals strapped and
their bags packed, God had them prepare a final feast.

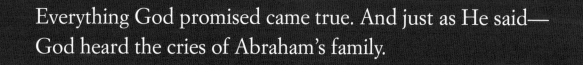

That night, while death itself roamed the streets of Egypt, the
blood of a spotless lamb marked God's people as His own.
And death passed over them.

"God has looked down on our humble estate; Let us rejoice in God our Savior! Let our souls magnify the Lord!"

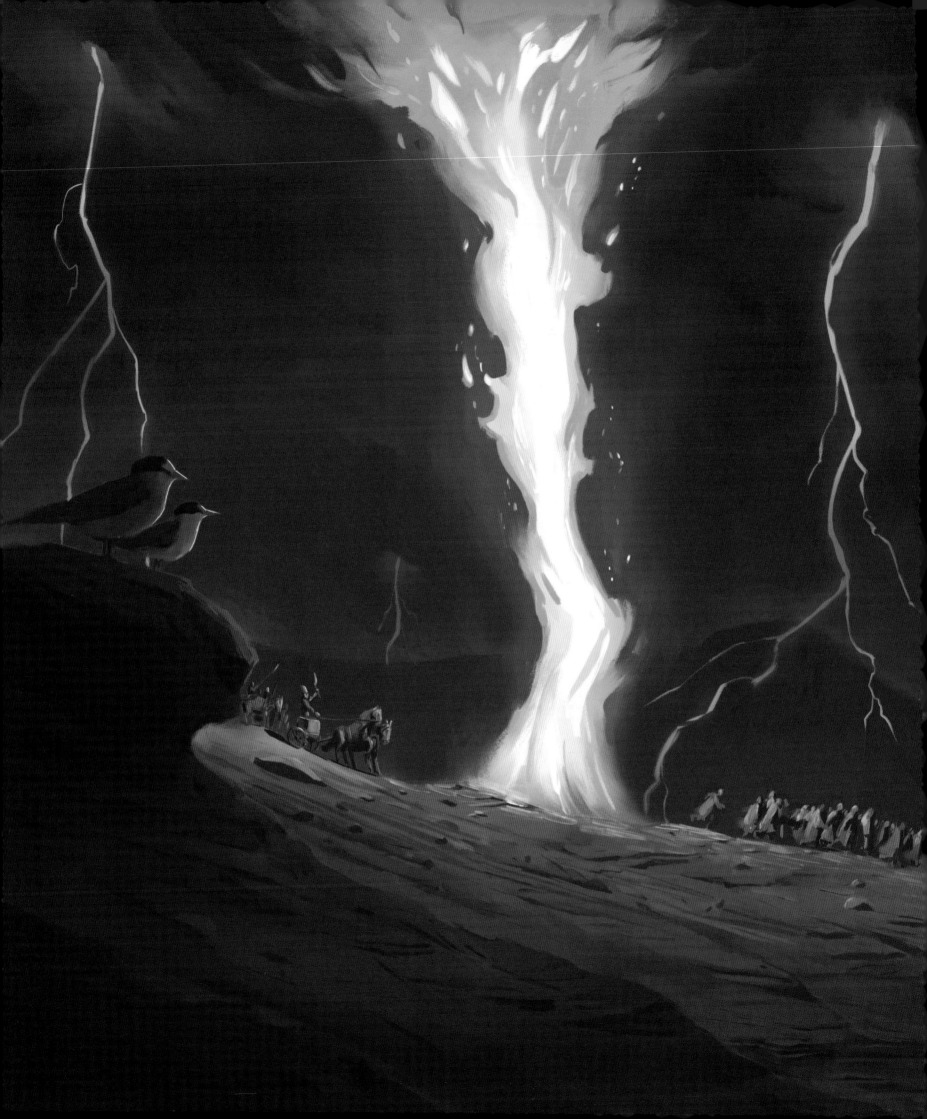

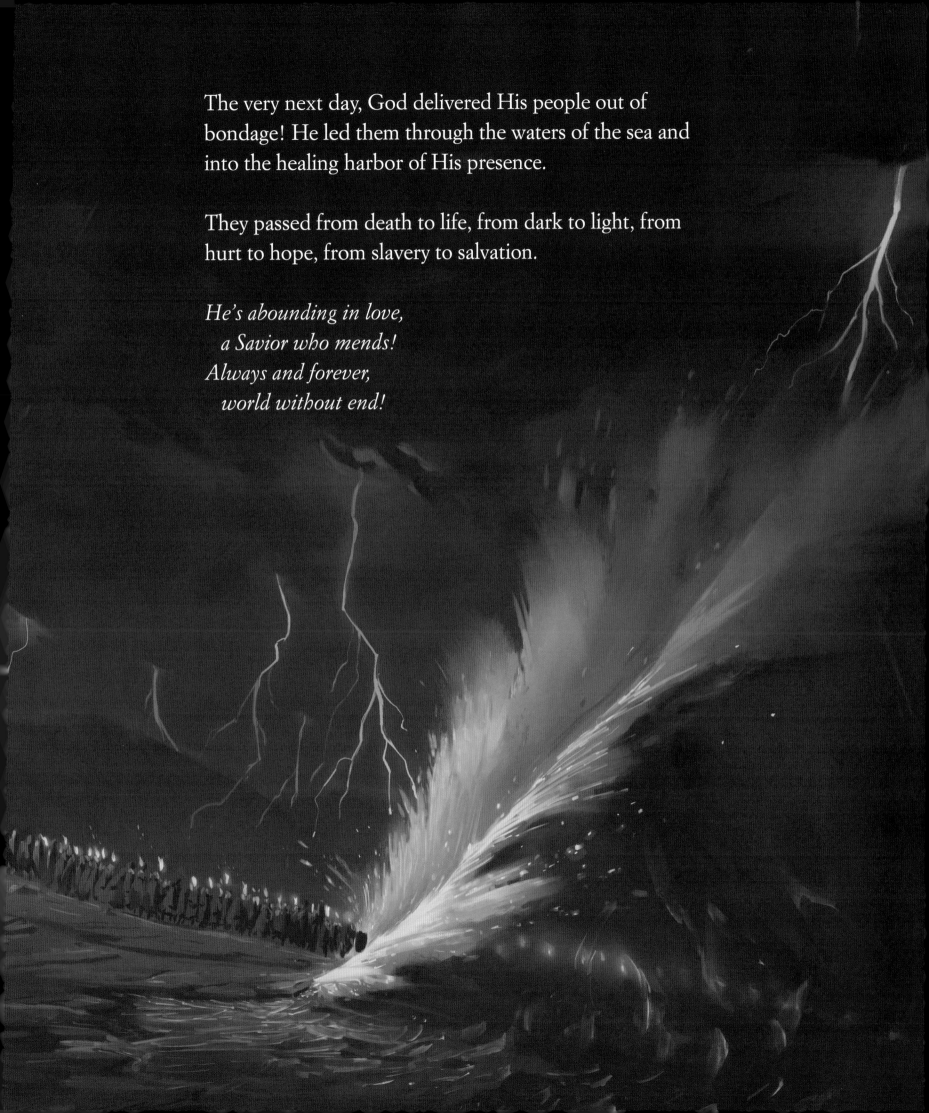

The very next day, God delivered His people out of bondage! He led them through the waters of the sea and into the healing harbor of His presence.

They passed from death to life, from dark to light, from hurt to hope, from slavery to salvation.

He's abounding in love,
  a Savior who mends!
Always and forever,
  world without end!

God gathered His newly rescued people at Mount Sinai so they could flourish in His presence!

But there was a big problem—Abraham's family was just as broken as the rest of the world. How could they dwell with their perfect Savior when they themselves were broken with sin and shame?

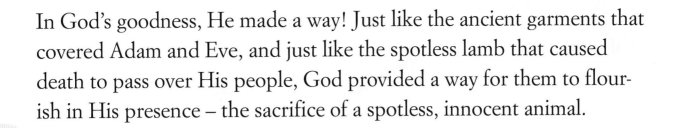

In God's goodness, He made a way! Just like the ancient garments that covered Adam and Eve, and just like the spotless lamb that caused death to pass over His people, God provided a way for them to flourish in His presence – the sacrifice of a spotless, innocent animal.

Would the blood of a lamb be enough to save?
   When will the sacrifice end?

How will God once and for all
   wash away *everyone's* sin?

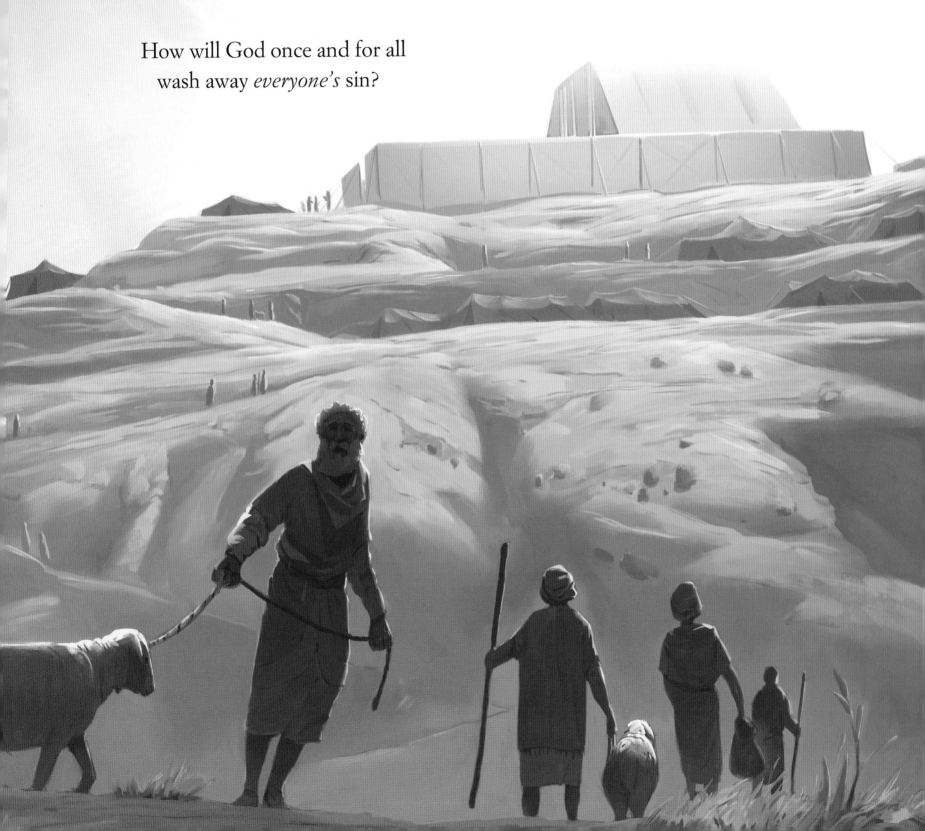

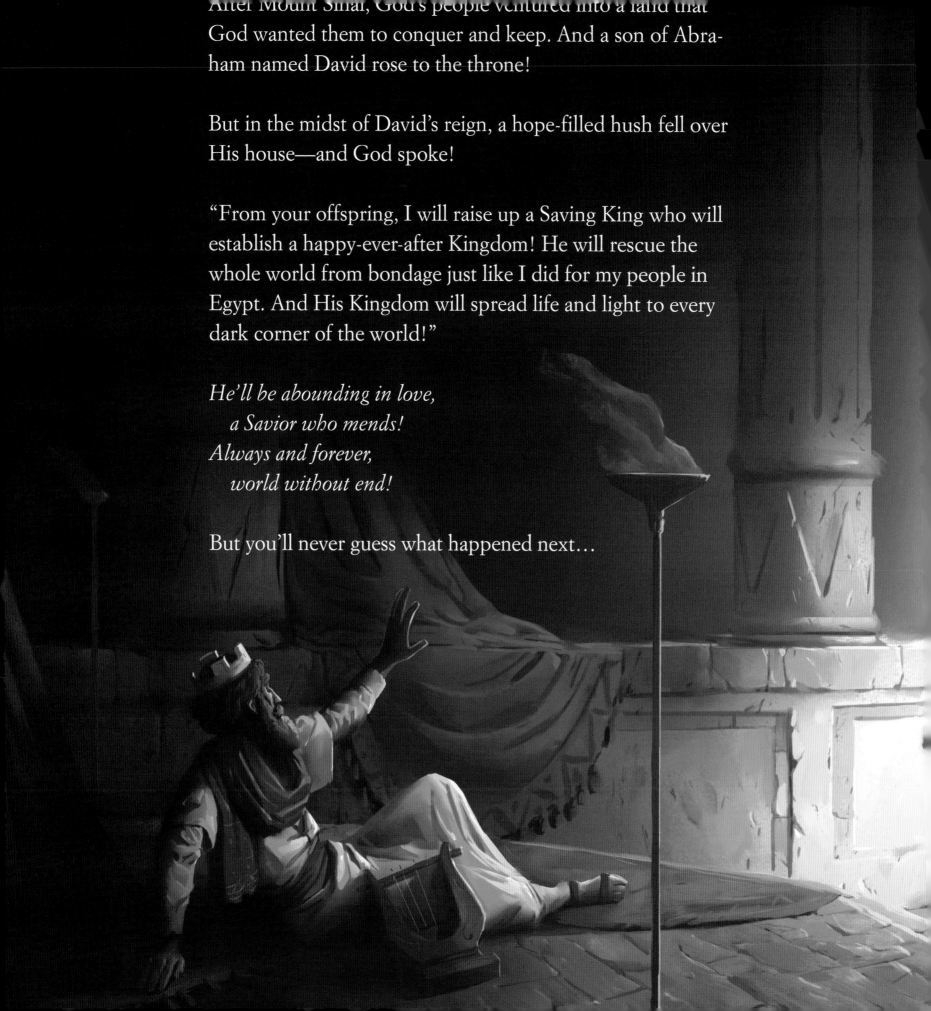

After Mount Sinai, God's people ventured into a land that God wanted them to conquer and keep. And a son of Abraham named David rose to the throne!

But in the midst of David's reign, a hope-filled hush fell over His house—and God spoke!

"From your offspring, I will raise up a Saving King who will establish a happy-ever-after Kingdom! He will rescue the whole world from bondage just like I did for my people in Egypt. And His Kingdom will spread life and light to every dark corner of the world!"

He'll be abounding in love,
  a Savior who mends!
Always and forever,
  world without end!

But you'll never guess what happened next…

Man's heart continued to fray.

Instead of celebrating, they sinned. Instead of showing faith, they fell away. Instead of acting like God's people, they acted like they didn't even know Him.

In their rebellion, they passed from life to death, from light to darkness, from hope to hurt, from salvation to slavery.

But as they passed into captivity, God's prophets left them with a word of hope –

"The Saving King is still coming! Though we fall, He will be faithful. Though we forget Him, He will remember us. Though our hearts fray — by His wounds we will be healed."

Hundreds of years passed by, and the prophets' words seemed to fade like ink on an old letter. But those who knew God knew better.

One still and sleepless night in the city of David, with sandals still strapped and bags strewn about a manger, a distant daughter of Eve and a great-grandson of Abraham waited in wonder. A hush fell over heaven and nature...

This was the new beginning – the fresh start God had promised!

The Saving King was born, and all creation sang!

"Mighty God! Prince of Peace!
    Who saves from death and sin!

Jesus has come! Our Saving King!
    Forever and ever, amen!"

"God has looked down on our humble
estate—Let us rejoice in God our Savior!
Let our souls magnify the Lord!"

"Behold, the Lamb of God
who takes away all our sins!"

He gave us His body and blood
in order to heal and to mend.

For God so loved the world
that He gave His only Son.

A final Lamb to die
so death could be undone.

The One who was True Life and Light
    was not held by the grave!

He rose to life, then rose on high
    to His forever reign!

All the brokenness of creation that started with Adam—the pain,
the sin, and the sadness—was bound up, forgiven, and healed in
the life, death, and resurrection of Jesus the Saving King!

He's abounding in love,
    a Savior who mends!
Always and forever,
    world without end!

After Jesus rested on His heavenly throne, He sent His Spirit to seek and save all His people from sin!

He leads us through the waters of baptism into the healing harbor of His Kingdom.

He carries us from death to life, from dark to light, from hurt to hope, from slavery to salvation!

Now, His Spirit-filled church follows Him to the ends of the earth, baptizing the broken into the name of the Father, the Son, and the Holy Spirit!

But God's heart is for much more—even much more than this!

One day, with a word from His mouth, He will banish darkness and death forever! And He will fill the whole earth with His healing presence!

He will wipe every tear from our eyes. There will be no more death or mourning or crying or pain, for the old order of things will pass away.

And all God's creation will sing forever to their Saving King!

"To Him who sits on the throne and to the Lamb be praise and honor and glory and power, forever and ever! Amen!"

He's abounding in love,
a Savior who mends!
Always and forever,
world without end!

The story you've just heard is meant to stay deep in your heart.
It's a *healing* story about a God who's mending what's falling apart.

Even in our darkest, most broken times, Jesus seeks us and saves us—He forgives us and sets us free to flourish! And you, dear child of God, are living in the days of the Saving King! And by the power of the Holy Spirit, He is inviting us into His saving mission!

So follow Him always,
   as He seeks and saves the lost.
May we always stand in wonder
   at the mercy of His cross.

He's abounding in love,
   a Savior who mends!
Always and forever,
   world without end!

BIBLE REFERENCE GUIDE

Creation & Fall: *Genesis 1–3:13 & 1 Corinthians 15:21–22*

The Promised Son: *Genesis 3:14–24*

The World Grew Darker: *Genesis 6–8*

A False Start (Noah): *Genesis 9*

Redemption Begins (Abraham): *Genesis 12:1–3; 15:12–14; 17:4–7*

The Destroyer & The Lamb of God: *Exodus 2:24–3:8; 12*

From Slavery to Salvation: *Exodus 14-15 & Psalm 77:15–20; 78:52–53; 136:10–15*

A Spotless Sacrifice: *Leviticus 1; 16:11–22 & Hebrews 9:11–14*

A Saving King (David): *2 Samuel 7 & Isaiah 9:6–7*

From Salvation to Slavery: *Isaiah 53:1–7 & Jeremiah 2; 29:10–14 & Ezekiel 11:19–20*

The Advent of the Saving King (Jesus): *Luke 1:46–55; 2:1–7*

Behold the Lamb of God: *John 1:29–34*

The Last Supper: *Mark 14:12–25*

The Spotless Sacrifice: *John 3:16; 19:16–42*

The Resurrection of the Saving King: *John 20*

From Slavery to Salvation: *Matthew 28:16–20 & 1 Peter 3:18–22*

New Creation: *Isaiah 65:17–25 & Revelation 21:1–8*